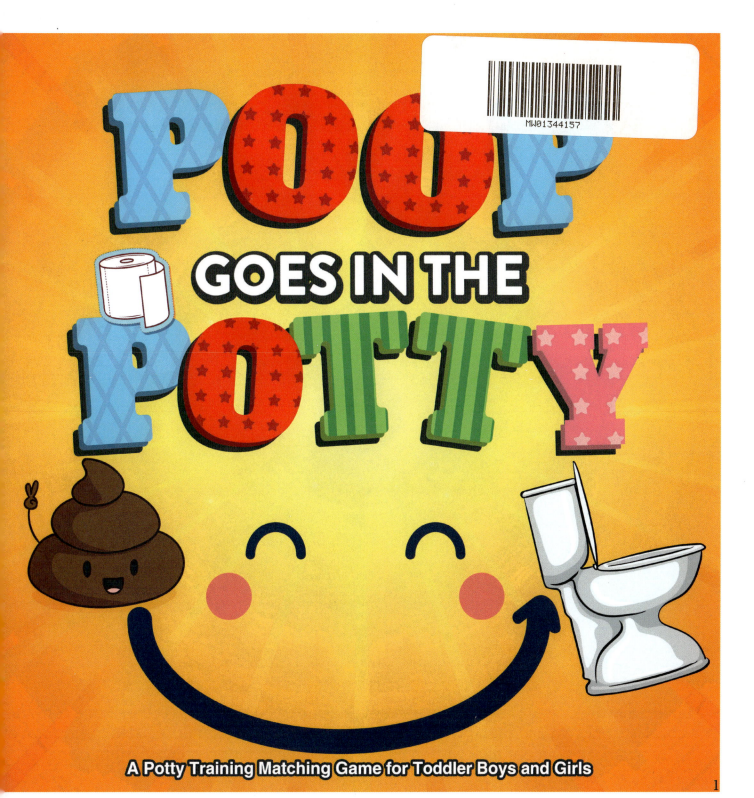

TM & Copyright© 2020 by Your Crazy Uncle™
ALL RIGHTS RESERVED.

Published in the United States. By purchase of this book, you have been licensed one copy for personal use only. No part of this work may be reproduced, redistributed, or used in any form or by any means without prior written permission of the publisher and copyright owner.

POOP GOES IN THE POTTY

Instructions

1. Grab a crayon or marker.

2. Match each item on the LEFT page to its correct pair on the RIGHT page.

3. Fill-out your Certificate of Completion!

 Easy as 1, 2, 3!

 For reference, all the correct pairs are located in the back of the book.

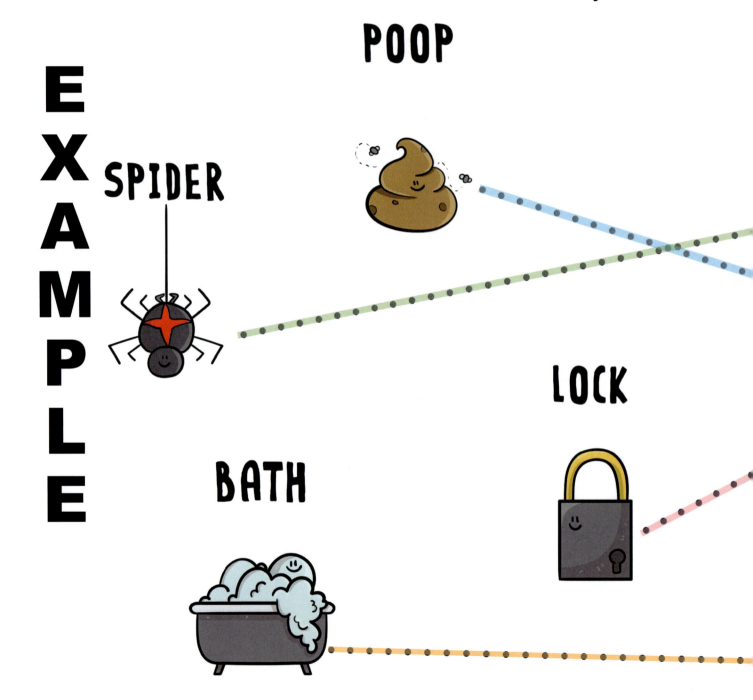

SPIDER WEB   KEY

EXAMPLE

POTTY

RUBBER DUCKY

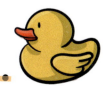

Match each item with its correct pair.

CAT

BASEBALL

COOKIE

POOP

POTTY

MOUSE

BASEBALL BAT

MILK

Match each item with its correct pair.

POOP

PENCIL

SALT

LOCK

PEPPER

KEY

POTTY

PAPER

Match each item with its correct pair.

BACON

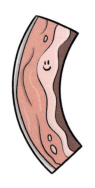

SHOE

POOP

DOG

EGG

POTTY

SOCK

BONE

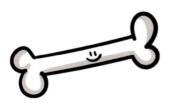

Match each item with its correct pair.

SPIDER

FORK

MITTEN

POOP

POTTY

KNIFE

SCARF

SPIDER WEB

Match each item with its correct pair.

WALLET

BIRD

SUN

POOP

POTTY

NEST

MOON

MONEY

Match each item with its correct pair.

PEANUT BUTTER

POOP

CHICKEN

FISH

FISHING POLE

POTTY

EGGS

JELLY

Match each item with its correct pair.

HAND

CHIPS

TOOTHBRUSH

POOP

FOOT

TOOTHPASTE

POTTY

SALSA

Match each item with its correct pair.

HAMMER

KING

POOP

TOILET

POTTY

TOILET PAPER

NAIL

QUEEN

Match each item with its correct pair.

POOP

RAIN

SOAP

KITTEN

WATER

BALL OF YARN

POTTY

RAINCOAT

Match each item with its correct pair.

FLOWER

LIGHT

POOP

MACARONI

CHEESE

POTTY

DARK

FLOWER POT

Match each item with its correct pair.

CEREAL

POOP

BEACH

SQUIRREL

MILK

NUT

POTTY

SEASHELLS

Match each item with its correct pair.

CAKE

MOVIE TICKET

LEFT

POOP

POPCORN

RIGHT

POTTY

CANDLES

Match each item with its correct pair.

POOP

BEE

SUGAR

BATH

POTTY

BEEHIVE

SPICE

RUBBER DUCKY

CERTIFICATE OF COMPLETION

Awarded to:

_____

FOR PRACTICING MATCHING PAIRS AND POTTY TRAINING

ANSWER KEY

Page 6-7
Baseball – Bat
Cat – Mouse
Cookie – Milk
Poop – Potty

Page 8-9
Pencil – Paper
Salt – Pepper
Lock – Key
Poop – Potty

Page 10-11
Bacon – Egg
Dog – Bone
Shoe – Sock
Poop – Potty

Page 12-13
Spider – Web
Fork – Knife
Mitten – Scarf
Poop – Potty

Page 14-15
Wallet – Money
Sun – Moon
Bird – Nest
Poop – Potty

Page 16-17
Peanut Butter – Jelly
Fish – Fishing Pole
Chicken – Eggs
Poop – Potty

ANSWER KEY

Page 18-19
Hand – Foot
Chips – Salsa
Toothbrush – Toothpaste
Poop – Potty

Page 20-21
King – Queen
Hammer – Nail
Toilet – Toilet Paper
Poop – Potty

Page 22-23
Soap – Water
Kitten – Ball of Yarn
Rain – Raincoat
Poop – Potty

Page 24-25
Flower – Flower Pot
Light – Dark
Macaroni – Cheese
Poop – Potty

Page 26-27
Cereal – Milk
Beach – Seashells
Squirrel – Nut
Poop – Potty

Page 28-29
Cake – Candles
Left – Right
Movie Ticket – Popcorn
Poop – Potty

Page 30-31
Sugar – Spice
Bee – Beehive
Bath – Rubber Ducky
Poop – Potty

Check out our next book!

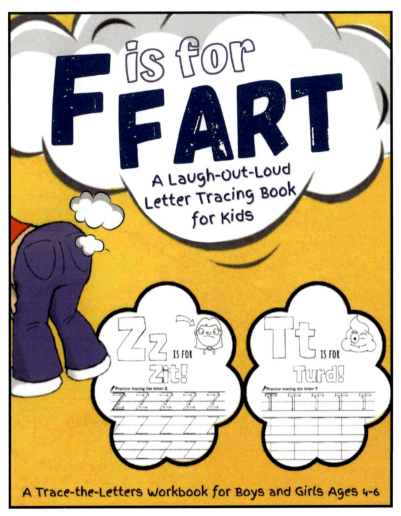

If you enjoyed this book, please leave a 5-star review on Amazon!

Made in the USA
Columbia, SC
21 November 2020